HEALING FROM NARCISSISTIC ABUSE:

HOW TO RECOVERY FROM NARCISSISTIC EXES AND PARENTS, TO CO-PARENT WITH A NARCISSIST AND MUCH MORE

Lindsay Travis

Table of Contents

Introduction

Research has revealed how much misinformation abounds about narcissism. Public perception of the subject is a hotbed of mismatching and oversimplified ideas; with a conflicting sense of what "healthy" self-enhancement is and what is not.

Much of the misguided rhetoric published online takes a black and white approach, as though narcissism is a pure and straight forward "label," rather than a range of healthy and unhealthy reactions and behaviors, triggered in 98% of people (including you, it is highly likely). These behaviors are present in varying intensities, for varying amounts of the time. Reactions depend not only on seemingly permanent, underlying thought- processes, but on what's going on in life, right now (and recently), that might be aggravating usually dormant self-esteem issues.

Narcissism exists on a spectrum from low levels to high. Some narcissism is healthy and is part of our normal responses to having our ego threatened, allowing us to maintain our sense of self without suffering from crushing shame and a sense of defeat. At the top of the scale is the personality disorder known as narcissistic personality disorder (NPD) characterized by a sense of superiority, a sense of importance and a deep need for admiration.

This book takes a more nuanced approach to the narcissistic scale. We won't simply be talking about how to deal with those that are diagnosable with NPD, but also about many narcissistic people who fit lower down on the spectrum and are relatable to most people. We'll attempt to decipher how narcissistic the person you are dealing with is, give you a better understanding of their thoughts, feelings and motivations, and help you determine whether you should cut them out of your life, or "manage" them to a greater or lesser extent.

In some cases, you might find it would be better for your wellbeing to continue a more limited relationship with them. Whether to cut off from a narcissistic mother, for example, is a hugely important decision that affects you for the rest of your life. You may have a narcissistic mother that is not diagnosable with NPD (for example, not overwhelmed with narcissistic responses most of the time, nor fitting most of the diagnostic criteria), but does display frequent damaging narcissistic behaviors that have severely impacted your "sense of safety" and trust in your relationship.

Here I will share examples of those who have found contentment by managing and restructuring the paradigm of their relationships with narcissistic people who are non-abusive.

Feeling angry, humiliated, or as though you want to help or change narcissistic people is only natural. This can be incredibly tough to come to terms with. This book focuses only on what you can do for yourself, including managing the boundaries of your relationship, and asserting yourself as an independent person in your own right.

The fundamental need of everybody encompassing an exceptionally narcissistic individual is to guarantee that they are caring for themselves, keeping up their own psychological and physical wellbeing and prosperity, before taking care of the narcissist. The narcissist's wellbeing ought to never take need over anybody else's, whatever endeavors they make to control others into caring for their necessities before their own. Similarly, to how we're told to fix our oxygen mask before helping any other individual on a plane, you should particularly recall this methodology when managing narcissistic privilege. On the off chance that this must be accomplished by cutting contact, this might be a course you have to take.

In the case of psychological, emotional, or physical abuse, the answer of what to do next is simple. No one ought to be in a position where they are enduring maltreatment on account of another, but stopping the abuse by leaving the situation is the main game plan to take. If you can't leave, this book will assist you with exploring your choices about how to deal with the circumstance, to place yourself in an increasingly ensured position where your prosperity is less on the line.

You may find that a narcissistic person in your life is not abusing you but is negatively impacting you in some other way- through guilt, manipulation, bullying- or simply using you for their own means.

Chapter 1

Defining Narcissistic Personality Disorder

In order to discuss narcissistic abuse, we must first learn about the basic characteristics of a narcissist and how they manifest in their relationships with other people.

Numerous individuals will be amazed to discover that there are a few diverse subtypes and indications of narcissism. For instance, a narcissistic character can be cerebral or physical. The cerebral narcissist is the individual who acknowledges they are intellectually fundamentally more talented and sharper than each other individual. They look down on others and take part in their propensity that all they bring to the table intellectually will be better than the others' duties, whether or not it's an idea or methodology at work or how best to complete an obligation at home or in school.

The cerebral narcissist is tied in with intriguing others with their psychological ability and may frequently overstate or even make up stories from their lives to expand this response from others. The underlining segment of the narcissist's conduct is self-love. They revere themselves, yet they are likewise broke with regards to getting acclaim from others too. They will put others down if it makes them look better in every other person's eyes decisively.

Then you have the somatic narcissist, who is basically just madly in love with their aesthetic qualities. They are generally very meticulous about their appearances and will do anything to maintain their looks. They are in love with their own reflections and see no faults when they look in the mirror. Think of the guy at the gym who seems to live there, constantly looking at his reflection and showing off for everyone around him. Whenever he sees someone else who looks good, he may go out of his way to demonstrate his superiority in some way. Now, this isn't enough to go on to concretely label someone a narcissist, but it would definitely be familiar territory in terms of how a somatic narcissist might spend his time.

Okay, so we have these two overarching categories of narcissism. Now, let's talk a bit about the four different subtypes of narcissist personalities. These subtypes may be discussed using slightly different terminology in different mediums, but they are broadly uniform when we talk about the different types.

The first subtype is called overt narcissism. Overt narcissism describes a person who is narcissistic and openly displays this personality type. The overt narcissist is who most people think of first when anyone mentions the term narcissism. He is very loud and riotous about his achievements. He will utilize weapons like disgracing and ridiculing others to make himself look better than every other person, particularly when he feels like her status is being compromised. The clear narcissist doesn't stop for a second to make a move against others straightforwardly or support their inner self with no respect for how it influences others. This is because one of the essential principles of narcissism is a general absence of compassion for other people.

In their minds, there is no one more important than themselves, therefore, whatever they need to do to help themselves is perfectly fine, even if it means stomping all over others. This is often one of the first ways people recognize a narcissist; there is a blatant disregard for others that crosses over into inappropriate and hurtful territory, and they don't even try to hide it because there is zero feelings of shame or empathy. The overt narcissist will feed off of other people's positive reaction to their behavior, making them feel even more entitled to treat others how they want. They are the classic bully and may attract others as a kind of entourage simply because of the confidence and power they exude.

The second subtype of the narcissistic personality is called covert narcissism. This is an interesting one and probably quite controversial, depending on whom we're talking about. The covert narcissist is someone who hides their intentions and motivations behind a curtain of goodwill and humanitarianism. They contribute to charities, volunteer, help friends in need, but they do so with as much spotlight on them as they can conjure. They want to be seen being "good people" because this feed their self-image of basically being a saint who can do no wrong. They relish the praise they receive from others, people telling them they are so nice and kind and generous when all they really care about is making themselves look good.

The third subtype and one of the most damaging to victims is the seductive narcissist. This applies to both romantic relationships and nonromantic relationships and refers to the emotional manipulation that takes place in order to tie a person to the narcissist individual through a toxic emotional addiction that is first cultivated through a showering of affection over time, and then suddenly withdrawn. The seductive narcissist is skilled at making his victim feel like they are the most important person in the world to him. He may give gifts and spend lots of money on dates and talk openly about his emotions, feign vulnerability and sincerity, then, once the victim feels attached, will suddenly withdraw, pulling his victim along behind him. This is an especially cruel situation because the victim is being used completely for the sole purpose of the narcissist's pleasure and self-worship. He may not have feelings at all for his victim, but simply enjoys having someone tethered to him under false pretenses. It is a sickening and deeply hurtful experience for the victim once they figure out what is going on if they ever do.

The final subtype is also one of the more damaging types and is the vindictive narcissist. Similar to the overt narcissist, the vindictive narcissist will be quite open with their narcissistic personality traits, but in addition, the vindictive narcissist is set on destroying and tearing down others. This is how they feed their need to rise above everyone else. Their victims could be family members, romantic partners, coworkers, or anyone else they come to view as "in their way" somehow. Their methods for tearing down and destroying other people include all types of emotional and psychological manipulation; whatever works best. They may plant insidious rumors about others in an effort to get people to hate one another or talk about people behind their backs in order to manipulate others' opinions of them. They are the playground bullies who love seeing those they deem weak cry and beg and get emotional. This makes them feel superior and justified in what they do.

Chapter 2

Signs and Symptoms of the Narcissistic Personality Disorder and Their Traits

I t is not easy to recognize a narcissistic person if you do no pay attention to your environment. The ability to recognize narcissism starts with self-awareness. Before you can recognize the actions and emotions of a narcissist, you must be able to recognize your own emotions. The ability to recognize and manage your own emotions and those of others is referred to as Emotional Intelligence EQ. In psychology, we refer to people who have the ability to study and manage other people's emotions as high EQ individuals. High EQ individuals are not easy to manipulate. Narcissists prey on individuals who lack emotional intelligence. Individuals with low EQ are easy to manipulate. They can be swayed from their ideological principles and are often found to be followers of others.

With that in mind, if you are keen and pay attention to everything around you, it is easy to spot narcissism. You can recognize narcissism by observing someone's daily actions, paying attention to their visions and dreams, observing their perception of others, observing their reaction to emotional issues among others.

Narcissists Are Highly Reactive to Criticism and Opposition

They react explosively to matters that others would not. If you realize that someone does not accept criticisms, correction, or anything that sounds negative, you should start observing their actions closely. It is a fact that few people enjoy negative feedback. However, even though most people

do not like negative feedback, the reaction of a narcissist is explosive other than resistance.

Narcissists perceive themselves as being perfect and do not accept any comments or suggestions that might indicate otherwise. If you ask a narcissist a question that may reveal their weaknesses, they are quick to lie to protect themselves from showing weaknesses. This behavior of narcissistic individuals has been described as the Narcissist Dilemma.

This is because narcissists are often in a dilemma on whether to show their true personality and accept being weak or wear a fake personality and never accept their weaknesses. It is believed that the main reason why most narcissists are so defensive is that they hold fears and weakness that they do not want other people to see. In fact, narcissists have low self-esteem than they want the world to believe.

Display Low Self Esteem

Unless you are emotionally intelligent, you might never be able to read the low self-esteem among narcissists. They strive to cover their self-esteem with an over-glorified personality. Matter of fact, narcissists mostly brag about areas of life where they are the weakest. You will find a person who lacks wealth associating with the wealthiest people in the world. In their mind, they are ashamed of being poor. They do not want to be associated with poverty and therefore, they cover that by bragging about having money. They will associate everything they own with wealth and class. They purport only to buy the high-end products and do not think anyone else could own an item more valuable than theirs. All these factors act as a mark of their low self-esteem.

In relationships, they may turn violent and accuse the other partner of cheating without evidence. Most narcissist partners only turn violent due to paranoia and not because they have been cheated on. If a narcissistic person thinks that he/she is not worthy of having someone as a life partner, they will threaten and try to instill fear into that person. In reality, it is the narcissist who is afraid of being left alone.

Narcissists use fear, intimidation, and abuse to cover their low self-esteem. Although they never agree to have low self-esteem, they may confide in a friend or a person who is too close.

Most narcissists have an inner personality that they strive to hide.

Some narcissists develop narcissistic personality due to traumatic events in their childhood. They remain in childhood mentality for a long time and act to defend their personality from being exposed. They are usually afraid of facing their childhood fears and letting go of something that might be holding them back. To be able to spot the weakness and low self-esteem in a narcissistic person, you must be very attentive. You must pay attention to every word they say and action they take. Once in a while, they will give out words of regret and remorse.

Narcissists Are Excessively Self-Righteous and Defensive

Narcissists have a never-ending need to defender their actions. They are individuals who do things that might be termed as wrong and still find a way of defending them. For this treason, narcissists do not take criticism. They are pretentious; self-exaggerated, stubborn and self-protective. Every word that comes out of their mouths goes towards self-defense. Even when they are in a group, they tend to distinguish themselves from the group mistakes; however, they are quick to take glory for the success of the group. Narcissists do not enjoy working in groups because they feel group members may not meet the standards set within their minds. When they work in groups, they are controlling and eventually lead to disagreements within a group.

Narcissists are only friendly to people who follow their ways or those who fear them. They do not make friends with individuals who challenge their line of thought. They have an insistent need to be right even when the facts do not add up. Interestingly, they pay too much attention to whatever they do to ensure that it is done perfectly. When they encounter failure, they express rage and anger to everyone. In the workplace, they are quick to blame other workers for errors and mistakes.

In their words, there is no known vocabulary for an apology. They will never use the word "I am sorry" even when it is clear that they have made a mistake.

Easily Angered

The reaction of narcissists to other people's words, opinions, and actions is the most obvious clue of narcissism. Narcissists are known as highly sensitive individuals due to their fragile personality. They are angered by issues that may be termed as none issues by someone else. Their anger is mostly driven by words or actions that seem contrary to their ideologies. However, this type of reaction is also displayed in persons with other personality disorders. For instance, Boarder line personalities and highly sensitive individual display anger when challenged.

With narcissists, their anger is derived from the fact that challenges may either show them as weak or may prevent them from achieving their target. In which cases, most narcissists strive to cover their weaknesses by being dominant.

If a narcissist person is interested in a sexual partner, for instance, it is easy to tell their narcissistic personality by rejecting their terms. Even the seducer narcissists still fall victim to anger. The best way to recognize seducer narcissists is to frustrate their efforts continually.

Seducer narcissists are usually patient to some extent; however, as time goes by, they get impatient and start displaying wrath. Any actions that may make him/ her look weak or unworthy will trigger anger. When angry, narcissists are either abusive physically or emotionally. They will start with threats and then turn violent.

Lack of Empathy

If you find yourself working or dating someone who lacks empathy, you need to start trading carefully. In the beginning, they may show concern to you and be very helpful. However, the clue lies in how they treat other people. Look to see if the person shows the same

empathy to family members such as his brothers or sisters, mother or father. The way a person treats other family members will show their true personality. Most narcissists will never introduce their partner to family members or friends. If you are in a relationship with a person who cannot introduce you to friends or family members, start reading the red flags. Being around family members will bring out the true character of a person. A person who is easily angered might pretend when they are with you but will easily burst out to a brother. Most narcissistic individuals do not have good relationships with other family members.

Selfishness

Selfishness is a language that dominates the life of narcissists. During the early stages, they may pretend to give you everything you want. The best way to know if they are really selfless or just laying the trap, look at their actions towards other people. Their actions towards other people depict their true personality. When a person is in love or obsessed with someone, he/she may offer favorable treatment. However, the treatment slowly fades away and the true character of a person creeps in.

Secretive Characters

Narcissistic individuals are highly sensitive and secretive. The first clue to understanding the language is a quest to find out their true personality. When you try asking personal questions and looking for proof, narcissistic individuals quickly get defensive. Narcissists thrive on lies. Keep on pushing to know the truth about their past; previous relationships, family life and so on. Such inquiries should be made at the early stages before a narcissist completely take control of your mind.

Narcissists Project Qualities, Traits, and Personalities They Don't Embrace

In most cases, narcissists display qualities that are obviously not part of their fabric. Because they believe that if they continuously say they are good or loving, they will hide their true personality from the public. Most narcissists never come to a point of accepting their true personality. They will associate themselves with charismatic leaders and other individuals who are successful. In reality, their true identity is kept inside. If you are keen, you will easily notice that they say they are something they are not.

Essentially, the characters they pick help them to devalue and denigrate others. They will focus on other people's flaws and point out mistakes so that no one will focus on them. They believe that if they point out weaknesses in other people, they stand out as righteous.

Narcissists are quick to judge and always find a way of getting something bad out of everyone around them. This way, they focus all the negative energy to other people in a bid to protect their own personalities.

Understanding the personality of a narcissist is not easy if you are not keen. They are so good at hiding their true identity. Sometimes, they may use manipulation while in some cases, they will use force. Being caught in either situation is not good. Most narcissists usually start with mental manipulation. If they find that you can easily fall prey to their charm, they will keep the other symptoms hidden. However, if you turn out to be emotionally intelligent than they thought, they turn to physical abuse. You must be careful to protect yourself from all forms of narcissistic abuse. If you allow narcissistic abuse to continue for a long time, you eventually get

brainwashed and lose your ability to make sound decisions. Narcissistic abuse victims take years to recover and some never recover to the fullest. It is your personal responsibility to protect yourself from such individuals by being observant. Read the signs early enough and separate yourself from their line of thought.

Chapter 3
Understanding Narcissist:

Different Types of Narcissist

There are many different kinds of narcissists out there while reading these descriptions, stay mindful of the fact that these types are not fixed; a narcissist can evolve from one type into another, or even embody a unique blend of two or more types.

The Grandiose Narcissist

The grandiose or exhibitionist narcissist is the kind of person that we typically think of when we imagine a narcissist cliché. Generally speaking, they are extremely vain, condescending and arrogant, bold and charismatic, bombastic, and unashamed of their quest to acquire limitless power and prestige.

They are often so audacious in their narcissistic statements and behaviors that some will presume they are sarcastic or comedic when they are, in fact, being quite genuine. People may laugh it off when this person mocks those that they consider beneath them, or launches into a monologue of self-praise, thinking that this is a show put on for the sake of entertaining others, ironically failing to see that this is the narcissist's honest expression of personal opinion. Unfortunately, reactions of laughter or silent acceptance can serve to reinforce the narcissist's inflated sense of self-importance, as they interpret these as signs of agreement or approval.

Grandiose narcissists also tend to have a childlike lack of self-awareness, choosing behaviors that virtually scream, "Look at me! Look at me!" They are usually comfortable speaking highly of themselves while belittling others with such brazen confidence that one might wonder if they have never been taught that such behavior is considered rude.

This narcissistic type is likely to have the least shame in expressing their egocentric attitudes; this may be due to their genuine belief that they are obviously and strikingly better than everyone around them, and the accompanying assumption that this flamboyant pea-cocking is what others expect of them. For example, if a member of a foreign country's royal family met you but refused to shake your hand or make eye contact, you might accept their display of arrogance, in light of their title. A grandiose narcissist might struggle to understand why you wouldn't extend the same courtesy and respect to them. Though you may see yourself as more or less their equal, they believe themselves to be superior to you and everyone else, so their haughtiness and vanity are justified in their minds.

The Closet Narcissist

The closet narcissist is also called a "covert" narcissist. They have the same competitive, defensive, and shame avoidant mindset as any other narcissist type, but they express it in a stealthy way, flying under the radar. While a grandiose narcissist can be loud and showy, using bravado to mask their insecurities, the closet narcissist's preferred tactic is silence. This isn't a submissive or reticent silence; it is pointed and deliberate. While keeping their lips sealed, they are able to assert their status and superiority by judging others and ever refusing to make themselves vulnerable to similar judgment.

While the grandiose narcissist never misses a chance to hog the spotlight, the closet narcissist feels conflicted about their thirst for attention. They may have been raised in a household with another grandiose narcissist who would not tolerate competition; alternatively, they might have been raised to see any explicit bid for attention as tacky or undignified and therefore learned to become an expert at seeking attention in stealthy, underhanded ways. They commonly use snobbery to belittle others, looking down their noses at them rather than explicitly insulting them with words.

Self-image is often deeply important to them, but the closet narcissist would be reluctant to talk about this or let others see how much work goes into manufacturing the face, body, and dress they present to the exterior world. For example, a closet narcissist could become obsessed with exercise, perfecting their body shape through hours and hours of work at the gym each week – but when offered a compliment on their sculpted figure, they would not want to admit that it took effort on their part, preferring instead to pretend that the shape is natural and easy for them to carry. Or, they might admit to the hard work but claim they were motivated by health or happiness, rather than a desperate need to be admired.

In short, a closet narcissist is a master of disguise, using feigned humility, shyness, or a charitable demeanor to mask the self-centered motivations behind all of their actions. They may not be likely to brag about their achievements, financial successes, or romantic conquests, and they might not draw attention to themselves through physical grooming or dynamic, showy behaviors; instead, this type is more likely to seek attention from others in the form of sympathy or pity. Rather than drawing attention to their own good looks, skills, or talents, they might spend conversations belittling or invalidating the achievements and appearances of other people, with the silent implication of personal superiority. At a dinner party, the grandiose narcissist might feel no shame in claiming the seat at the head of the table in someone else's home, and helping themselves to the first and largest serving of food; the closet narcissist wouldn't take either of these actions, but instead might become offended and resentful of the fact that these courtesies weren't offered to them automatically.

Alternatively, the closet narcissist might define their self-worth and feel special based on their proximity to something unique, desirable, and unattainable – or their relationship with a person who embodies the same qualities. For example, a closet narcissist may not be particularly boastful or ostentatious about it, but choose to dress in elite designer brands from head to toe, hoping that only other special people of a similar degree of importance might recognize them as a member of the same club. Or, they might find their source of superiority by befriending celebrities or powerful politicians. Covert narcissists tend to make excellent assistants to high-powered bosses, talent managers, and behind-the-scenes orchestrators; just beyond the reach of the spotlight, they can stand beside the star and pull all the strings from a comfortable, well-shielded position.

They struggle to maintain personal relationships or start them since they aren't as confident, charismatic, or overtly charming as their grandiose counterparts. When they do build any type of close relationship, though, they often develop a two-faced demeanor, presenting one personality to the outside world and exhibiting just the opposite when alone with a "loved" one.

Like the grandiose narcissist, the closet narcissist can develop their personality disorder as a response to narcissistic abuse in childhood. While they possess a deep understanding of the grandiose and malignant narcissists' mindsets and could offer tremendous insight to the recovery community, they choose the path of defensiveness over empathy, embracing the idea that "if you can't beat them, you might as well join them." Since they spend so much time within their heads, a closet narcissist may be the most likely of the three to seek treatment, healing, and change eventually, but they will only be able to do so if they are pushed to admit their vulnerability. Otherwise, their deeply self-conscious mindset becomes a self-reinforcing prison that can pull them further and further away from the connection to reality over time.

The Malignant Narcissist

Malignant or toxic narcissists are rarer than both the grandiose or covert types, which is lucky for the rest of us. If you've ever known a true malignant narcissist, you understand what a volatile and destructive force this personality disorder can be. People who earn this title typically suffer from a combination of narcissistic personality disorder along with one or more others, such as antisocial personality disorder, manic or compulsive behavioral issues, paranoia, or sadistic inclinations. They are often the easiest narcissists to recognize, as they are usually unable to achieve the same degrees of success that grandiose or covert narcissists can grasp.

Without real evidence of their superiority, in the form of money, status, power, educational degrees, or social support, it can be overwhelmingly obvious to others that the malignant narcissist has an unrealistic opinion of their own importance. It is not obvious to the malignant narcissist, though.

Malignant narcissists tend to see the world through a lens of dichotomies, the most important of which is "me versus everyone and everything else." They have trouble understanding grey areas or multifaceted concepts, preferring to define everything as either good or bad, right or wrong, love or hate, yes or no, now or never. They also have an impulse to turn everything into a competition, applying the logic of scarcity to circumstances where it isn't necessary; for example, at a pizza party with more food and more seating than is needed to accommodate everyone's needs, the malignant narcissist might get bent out of shape over who takes the largest slice of any particular pie, or who claims the seat that they consider most optimal, even though there's more than enough to go around.

They often create mountains out of molehills and spin up trouble out of thin air. They see chaos as the stage upon which they perform best, providing ample opportunity for them to manipulate others and secure further power for themselves. Regardless of any social or financial stability, they secure for themselves as adults. They are mentally stuck in survival mode; this means that when they perceive another person as a threat, they can quickly and easily leap to a disproportionate self-defensive gesture.

While both the grandiose and covert narcissist aims to maintain a certain level of respectability in regards to their reputation and therefore keep their unsavory attitudes reigned to some degree, the malignant narcissist appears to be unmoved by the disapproval of others, and uninhibited in their expressions of negativity and egocentricity. For example, when on the receiving end of a public slight, all three types of narcissist would feel the impulse to retaliate; however, the grandiose narcissist might be compelled to consider their audience and exact vengeance in the form of a witty comeback, or to wait until a more private moment to express their rage; the covert narcissist would be similarly driven to save face in public, and would perhaps be most likely to seek revenge by spreading rumors, or finding an anonymous way to get back at their foe. By contrast, the malignant narcissist would be most likely to react immediately and escalate the conflict through yelling, name-calling, and perhaps even physical violence.

The malignant narcissist is the most dangerous of the three types. At times, their behavior can be indistinguishable from that of the criminally psychopathic. They see no problem with causing pain for others as a means to an end; in some cases, they may even derive pleasure from causing emotional or physical harm to their victims, enjoying the rush of sadistic power it provides for them.

Chapter 4

Narcissism and Abuse

I f one word had to sum up all of the tactics you will encounter when dealing with a narcissist, it would be this: diversionary. Every single word and action you use to question their behavior will somehow be turned against you and leave you questioning your sanity.

Diversions

These tactics are not limited to just narcissists. People with other maladaptive disorders like psychopathy and those with antisocial leanings also use them. The difference is that with the narcissist, they are used far more often and over a longer period of time.

Gas lighting

Taking its name from the famous play "Gas Light" published in 1938, gas lighting refers to the phenomenon wherein the abuser seeks to distort the victim's sense of reality. They may do this by saying "you're imagining things" or "that didn't happen." The goal is to convince the victim that the victim's version of reality is wrong, while the narcissist's version is correct. Gas lighting is an extremely unnerving tactic that, when done right, will cause you to distrust yourself and have you entirely at the mercy of your abuser.

Gas lighting takes place in stages and the level of reality distortion slowly increases. It starts out with something small and then the level slowly ratchets up. A lot of victims are not aware of this taking place since to a normal person, this sort of thing seems almost supernatural.

Feelings of going mad and questioning your reality are quite normal when this happens since the victim begins to wonder whether she can trust herself. At first, victims have the energy to question the alternate version of events as put forward by the abuser but over time, their energy wears out and they simply give in.

The most effective form of gas lighting requires a kernel of truth within it. More often than not, this kernel is provided by the victim himself. For example, when the narcissist turns cold and unresponsive and begins to behave in a suspicious manner, a gas lighter will accuse the victim of being too possessive and paranoid. He'll be accused of being suspicious, and the abuser will threaten to walk out on the relationship, thus ensuring that the victim pleads for them to return.

Staying grounded is the key to avoiding gas lighting. Leaning on a support network of friends and trusted people is the best way to cope. It also helps to write a record of events, but make sure this doesn't fall into your abuser's hands since it will be turned against you.

Projection

Projection is a common psychological phenomenon wherein someone projects their experiences and conclusions onto someone else. For example, if you encountered a vicious dog during your childhood, you may view every single dog you meet later in life as vicious, even if the dog simply wants to play and be friendly with you.

Everyone engages in projection in one way or another, but the narcissist uses projection as a weapon of manipulation. The victim will find themselves being accused of all sorts of shortcomings which are really the abuser's own. The victim will find themselves accused of being a liar or of being insecure, for example.

Every single accusation is a way of shifting the focus from the abuser's actions back onto the victim. If the victim accuses the abuser of being unfaithful, it is the victim who is accused of being too clingy. Combined with gas lighting, this soon leads the victim to question their sense of reality.

Ad Hominem Attacks

Ad hominem refers to a debate tactic where a person attacks their opponent instead of attacking the issue that they presented. This is quite often seen in political debates of any sort, but it is also prevalent when dealing with a narcissist. The slightest disagreement with a narcissist can set off a wave of arguments and fights that will leave you wondering where you even began and why this happened in the first place.

Ad hominem attacks invoke an emotional reaction in all of us since they are personal. The reason the narcissist will turn to this style of argument is that every disagreement you place in front of them is taken as a personal attack to their fragile sense of self.

Therefore, the only method of rebuttal is a personal attack, and the victim, without knowing what has happened, is forced into a situation where they need to defend points of argument that are nonsensical and completely unrelated to what was being discussed in the first place.

Exaggeration

Remember that a narcissist doesn't need to be the smartest person in the room. All they need to be is the most emotionally manipulative. Exaggerating anything about the victim or their statements is a surefire way of turning the argument against them and claiming the moral high ground.

Statements like "you're always clingy" or "you're doing this or that" are aimed at provoking an emotional reaction within the victim which causes the victim to retaliate. Once the retaliation takes place, it's simply a matter of playing the victim and pandering to the actual victim's sympathy.

Exaggeration is also used to attack the victim and to play up the victim's negative qualities in order to make the victim feel bad about themselves. Questioning the victim's intelligence and repeatedly highlighting past mistakes are ways of making the victim feel insecure and having them become more dependent on the abuser.

Conditioning

Conditioning refers to the entire set of behaviors and tactics that a narcissist will carry out in order to have their victims become more and more dependent on them. It occurs much like gas lighting in that it takes place over time as the narcissist slowly but surely gets the victim to associate their (the victim's) strengths and positive qualities with abuse.

Thus, the victim feels unhinged and turns to the closest person to them at the time, which happens to be the abuser. This gives the narcissist a lot of pleasure since it not only validates their belief that they're the most important person in the world but also panders to their heightened sense of self-importance.

Signs of conditioning include getting the victim to stay away from their former friends and getting them to mistrust their family, with whom the victim previously had a great relationship. In fact, any positive relationship of any kind is discouraged by the narcissist since this undermines their hold over the victim.

Stalking

Every so often the narcissist runs into a strong person who cannot easily be made into a victim. Either as a tactic to seduce them or as a retaliatory measure, the narcissist will resort to a smear campaign to bend opinion of the victim toward what they want. This is aimed at undercutting the social bonds the victim already has and leaving the victim at the mercy of the abuser.

This sort of toxic behavior can extend beyond an individual to even entire groups of victims as they get hounded socially from all sides. Gossiping about someone behind their backs, stalking their social media, and implying nasty things are all part of the narcissist's toolbox.

Triangulation

This is a particularly insidious tactic where the narcissist gets affirmation of their point of view, against their victim, by recruiting one of the victim's trusted sources, such as a friend or a family member. This leads the victim to believe further that the abuser must be correct since the third trusted person is also affirming this view.

In this particularly insidious tactic, a narcissist uses one of the victim's trusted sources, such as a family member or a friend, to further belittle the victim. The goal is to use the third source to convince the victim that the narcissist's negative view of the victim is accurate. This leads the victim to believe further that the abuser must be correct since the trusted third person is also affirming this negative view.

While there are situations where a victim is being triangulated by abusers on all sides, more often than not, it is the narcissist who is misrepresenting what the third person said and is twisting facts to support their narrative. Often, the third person, himself, is being triangulated using the victim. Common tactics to achieve this include telling the victim that the third person has said negative comments about the victim, when in fact, that is not the case. The goal is to distance the victim from that support person. One of the best ways to resist this tactic is to triangulate the abuser themselves by using a person who isn't under their influence and calling out their behavior. Most likely the abuser will lash out, but the triangulation you have achieved will help ground yourself in reality and see what is going on.

While the narcissist has his or her tactics, a lot of people still manage to fall prey to them, despite having full knowledge of all of this. Why is this so? Well, a lot of it has to do with the nature of the victim. Mind you, I'm not blaming the victim here but merely trying to say that the abuser often turns certain qualities the victim has against them.

Chapter 5

The Steps of Healing

Healing from narcissistic abuse is not easy by any means. It is not something that anyone ever really wants to discuss—they just want it to go away somehow. You may find that you have suffered from narcissistic abuse for far too long. You may have been taught early on that you are a victim, and because you are a victim, you deserve very specific treatment. You may find that as a victim, you are likely to be looked down upon. You may find that as a victim that you are pitied. However, no one likes to be pitied. No one wants to be pitied.

You can allow for the pity to end. All you have to do is shift your mindset. You have acted like, at the end of the day, you are going to be a victim and that you will need to change yourself somehow. You are going to change your mindset from being a victim to being a survivor. As a survivor, you made it through to the other end. You made it to where you were headed, and now you get to celebrate. When you make yourself the survivor instead of the victim, you change how you think about yourself. You remove that stigma of having been abused and having been beaten up in the past and instead allow room for growth.

We are going to go over several steps that you can use in order to heal yourself, one at a time. Remember, healing is a process. It will take time and effort, and the fact that you are taking this step in the first place is monumental itself. Now, let's go over those steps, one by one.

Acknowledge the Abuse

The first step toward healing is acknowledgment. You must acknowledge what has happened if you hope ever to be able to heal. That acceptance is critical. You must recognize and admit to yourself that the narcissist has hurt you in the past. You must recognize this so you can move forward. You may feel victimized and ruined at first—like the narcissist stole something precious from you. However, you are still a whole person. You are still able to have everything that you hoped. You are still able to recognize that you are a whole individual, capable of having likes and dislikes. However, within your story, you add to the narrative—you were abused in the past, but you have broken free and fled the area. In admitting this to your narrative, you not only admit that you have been hurt by the narcissist, but you have taken a monumental step toward healing.

You are finally admitting that there is a problem here in the first place when you acknowledge the abuse, and that is powerful. When you can acknowledge that it happened, you are stepping back. You are bracing yourself. You are preparing for exactly what you have to do, and you are willing to do it. You are ensuring that you will actually be able to cope with the situation because you are willing and able to acknowledge the abuse and begin to remove yourself from it, little by little. It may help in this part of the process, for you to write down the ways in which your partner was abusive in general. This can help you keep your resolve in the future when you may find that you are tempted to go back to the narcissist. Keep in mind that it takes an average of 8 times of leaving actually to stay gone. That means that it will take you time and energy to really stay gone and allow yourself to begin to heal properly. Healing is a difficult task, and you will need to allow yourself plenty of time and patience for it. If you can do that, you will be able to better yourself.

Have Patience for Yourself

After you have acknowledged that you have a problem, you must be willing to be patient with yourself. You must be willing to acknowledge the problem as soon as possible, as well as reconcile with the fact that you did not actually ask for any of this to happen. You must be patient with yourself during the healing process, reminding yourself that you did not deserve what you got and that you are going to be changing yourself and your mind, little by little.

The entire healing process is quite long and can appear daunting to some. It can take months, weeks, or even years before it happens in completion, and because of that, it is easy to begin getting upset or frustrated at the fact that you are still suffering or struggling. You may find that you deserve so much better than what you got, and this is true. However, there is little point in dwelling in these negative feelings. They are there, and they should be a reminder that you should stay away from the narcissist in the future, but at the end of the day, you must also recognize that you deserve forgiveness as much as anyone else does.

As you have the patience for yourself, remind yourself never to rush the process. It is next to impossible to forgive yourself overnight simply— this is why it can be so important for you to have patience. It will take time for you to develop your own forgiveness towards yourself, but you will eventually get it. It is just a matter of time at this point.

Forgiving Yourself

At this step, you should be willing to forgive yourself for the abuse that you endured and for allowing it to last as long as it did. In forgiving yourself, you should be making it a point to acknowledge that the abuse that occurred was not your fault. You may be angry about it or wish that it had never happened at all, and that is okay—you are entitled to your feelings. However, you must also be willing to take away the blame from yourself. You are not responsible for abuse happening to you. You have taken steps to begin to get away from the narcissist, and that is major on its own.

You may feel blindsided—like you should have known that the abuser was a narcissist. However, remind yourself that he is someone that is an expert at hiding his true self. You may feel like you are shocked that you put up with everything for as long as you did. Remind yourself that you did not just sit back without doing anything—you have been taking the steps you will need in order to reclaim your life. Recognize that you did not ask for any of this and remove your blame for it. Would you blame someone who got hit by a drunk driver for the accident when they did nothing wrong? No—so why are you blaming yourself? Why are you making it your own fault that you were abused and taken advantage of?

Let go of that blame in this step. Let it all out, whether through the use of any sorts of affirmations or anything else. You must be willing to let it go to progress.

Grant Yourself Time to Grieve

When you are finally beginning to heal from the narcissist, you may feel angry and sad. And then, you may feel frustrated and confused, and perhaps even some shame, at feeling so sad in the first place. After all, you were in love with a narcissist who wanted nothing more than to hurt you—why should you love or miss him?

The truth to this is one that you may not want to hear. The individual that you got to know is not the real person. The person that you loved was a pretense—a fake character created by the narcissist in order to win you over. All the narcissist needed to be someone that was willing to recognize the situation. When you recognize this, you are able to recognize that you have lost someone that was dear to you—it is almost like someone that you fell in love with has died. In a sense, he did—he will never be there with you again. That can be traumatic for anyone at all—you do not have to be involved with the individual to realize that.

For this reason, it becomes important that you give yourself the appropriate amount to grieve your loss. Usually, the loss will be grieved in five distinct steps. However, the steps do not always happen linearly. Healing is not linear at all—you can be fine one day and absolutely devastated the next. However, if you can give yourself the permission that you need, you can begin to grieve appropriately.

The first step to grief is denial; this is where you deny the idea that anything was wrong in the first place. Here, you are rejecting the idea that the narcissist is not who you think he is. You deny that the persona that you got to know is nothing more than a persona. You want to make sure that you can get back to your relationship as soon as possible and refuse to acknowledge that anything may be amiss.

Next comes anger. Here, you are furious about what has happened. You have become furious at the idea that you have lost someone. You are angry at the narcissist for messing around with your heart. You are furious because you were taken for a ride without even realizing it. You know that you were lied to, and that is devastating. You are angry and not afraid to show it.

The third is bargaining. This is a strange step. In this step, you choose to beg to get back to your relationship. You begin to wonder if you could get back to that life, complete with the ex, all because you are not quite ready to admit what is wrong and why you are so afraid of the situation.

You then go through step four: Depression. At this stage, you find yourself accepting the truth once and for all. You accept that the other person is not coming back. You need to be able to handle the situation for everyone involved to ensure that everyone. You try to make yourself deal with the feelings, but you just feel numb and empty.

Finally, you arrive at the final stage: Acceptance. At this point, you can finally accept what has happened. This does not mean that you must be entirely over what has happened—you are able to recognize that you were taken for a spin by someone that does not like or care about you, and that is painful to cope with. However, you know that it is what it is, and there is no changing it. That is powerful.

Create Support

The narcissist wants you to remain without any real contact with the outside world. You know that he says the opposite, but you have caught him looking through your computer history more times than you can count. You know that he is looking for what you have been doing lately—especially if you have been insisting on getting therapy in the first place. He is going to try to isolate you in any way possible, and if you have broken free, you still may feel isolated.

When you are able to create or join a support system, however, you are beginning to connect yourself with all sorts of other people that you know can help you. You will be looking to see if anyone in your surroundings will be able to help you keep your resolve firm and help you remain resolute in your decisions when you find a support network of other people who have suffered at the hands of a narcissist.

Chapter 6

Ending A Relationship with A Narcissist

The time is right for you to leave if you have undergone any emotional, mental, or physical abuse, if you have identified serious cycles of manipulation or narcissistic issues that never change, if you are sacrificing your power, integrity, success, and desires, or if you feel like you are being taken advantage of on a regular basis to support someone else's fantasies of who they are. There are a lot of ways that narcissism from within your relationship can affect your quality of life, your personal views, your self-worth, and more, and it is not worth it to stick around, hoping that your partner will change and be more what you need. They don't care about what you need. They will only ever care about what they need.

If you have tried for a long time to help your partner identify their issue and help them "heal" their problem to no avail, then it is time to let go and move on. It is important to recognize that you can never heal someone for them; they have to do the work to heal themselves. Being a supportive partner is always a good thing, but if you are familiar with how your patterns of support have enabled your narcissistic partner to stay in their preferred role and behavior patterns, then you need to admit that you are at the end the rope, so that you can heal on your terms and find a happier lifestyle.

The stages of detaching from your partner can go on for a while, as you begin to identify the issues and start to pull away, changing your role in the situation and recognizing your readiness to end things. It can be uncomfortable for your partner, who will make it uncomfortable for you as a result, and so understanding some of the stages that you will likely go through will help you prepare for moving on.

Detachment from a Narcissist: Stages

First Stage:

When the rose-colored glasses come off and you stop accepting blame, guilt, or shame in your relationship, you begin to resurface and "wake-up" to what has been going on. In the first stage, you are "seeing" more clearly all of the patterns, the covert and subversive ridicule, and all of the tools of manipulation to push you away and punish you and then pull you back in and adore you. This is the stage of awareness of the problem and the first shift that changes the situation.

Second Stage:

You may still have feelings for your partner at this point, even a seriously deep love bond, however, your usual desire to please them no matter what will begin to be replaced with the feeling of anger, and even resentment that they are so consistently and continuously demanding of your admiration, adoration, and pleasure. The love may still be there, but you are not so "naïve" anymore.

Signals of the Second Stage:

- Your partners lie no longer affect you and feel obvious and pathetic.

- You are no longer succumbing to the manipulation tools.

- You regain a sense of self-worth and feel you deserve to be treated better.

- You will begin to fight for yourself more and will create more conflict with your partner.

- You begin to regain and rebuild your self-confidence and self-esteem.

Third Stage:

Your confidence is being reborn, and you are feeling better about yourself and your choices. You may have already joined a support group at this time or started to see a counselor help your growth and are feeling more empowered emotionally and mentally. You can better focus on your wants and needs and can start to see how life would be if you are not involved with your narcissistic partner.

Signals of the third stage:

- You can't stand to be around your partner.

- You no longer feel an obsessive love or strong love bond.

- If they begin to push your buttons or act inappropriately, you will either have no reaction and not care or retaliate and lash out against them.

- Enjoying more time with friends, in support groups, engaging in classes, or group meet-ups that support your interests
- You will start to make decisions to support yourself without concerning yourself with your partner's preferences or interests.
- You will begin to make your move to let go and move on by planning out and getting your ducks in a row.

Fourth Stage:

This is the end of the relationship when your focus becomes facing your future without your partner. At this point, you may have cut the cords, moved out, separated, begun the divorce proceedings, etc. This is the stage when you will have cut them off and out of your life and when you can begin to feel new and like yourself again. You will not want anything to do with your partner, and in some cases, you may have to maintain some kind of contact (if you have children together).

The Overall Process of Letting Go and Moving On:

This process won't occur for anyone overnight. You can end up living in the cycles of one stage for a long time until you are resolved to move forward into the next stage. Getting stuck in these processes is highly common, and there is a way to help you ease through a little bit better so that you don't stay stuck for longer than you need to be.

As you begin to consider letting go and moving on, hang onto those thoughts and let yourself feed into them. You are allowed to imagine your life differently, apart from your partner, and it can help you to build steam and momentum if you continually consider the process of cutting cords and stepping forward. It helps to keep fueling your self-esteem and doing things that will help you support yourself in the process. Follow these steps to help:

1. Think about it. Let yourself fuel your exit with self-esteem building and thoughts about moving on. Build momentum so that you can keep revisiting why you are having these thoughts to begin with.

2. Use a journal or a notebook to write out all of the experiences you want to have, the life you want to live, the places you want to go, and where you want to be successful in your life. Start to write down and consider the kind of partnership and partner you would like to experience. You can even jot down all of the aspects of your current relationship and then make a comparison between what you have and what you want. Getting into the habit of journaling about you and what you want can help you to refocus your life goals and ambitions and further motivate you to let go of the relationship that is hurting your choices and chances for a healthy and successful life.

3. Reflect. Explore your relationship and ask yourself what part, or role, you have played in the experience. The narcissist may be manipulative, toxic, and cunning, but it certainly always takes two to tango, and so it might help you to be honest and identify what ways you have supported the toxicity of your relationship. How have you not lived up to your standards of love and life? How have you enabled this behavior? What can you do to shift these patterns? Spend time with these thoughts and truly reflect on your energy in the relationship. Write it down in your journal and begin to create

awareness about your role in the partnership. You don't want to fall for the narcissist again, and knowing where you fall for the traps can help you resist them in the future.

4. Find supportive literature. There are countless books out there that aren't just about overcoming a narcissistic relationship, but they are also about empowering yourself, finding the career of your dreams, learning new skills and hobbies, and so on. You can begin to reclaim your identity and your sense of pride and joy in your life by seeking out self-improvement books and literature that will empower you and give you strength.

5. Spend time with others. Connect with your family, friends, co-workers, support groups, etc., and talk about it. Feel free to be yourself around your network of loving and supportive people to help you feel that you are not going to be alone when you walk away and move forward.

6. Write a letter. You don't have to give the letter to your partner, but it can be a very therapeutic experience for you to write out a detailed account of your feelings, your anger, your sorrow, and how they have made you feel over the months or years. It is more for you than for them, and it can give you a chance to say what you were never allowed to say to their face.

7. Go ahead and feel. Cry, scream, roll around on the floor, and laugh as hard as you want to! Feel all of your feelings, and don't look for ways to distract yourself from how you are feeling. If you are feeling pain, anger, and fear in your relationship, don't bury the feelings;

honor them and tell yourself that you know why you feel that way. The more you acknowledge your true feelings, the more you will understand why you have them and what to do about it.

8. Get comfortable with your fears. It is okay to be afraid. Fear is a doorway to something we might not feel capable of achieving or something that feels unknown, and therefore, frightening. The more you allow yourself to sit with your fear and ask it questions, the better able you will be to overcome these fears. Repression and escape are what keep you locked in cycles and patterns that are unhealthy, such as the narcissistic partnership. You can wake up your fears so that you know what they are and what to do about them.

As you brace yourself to let go and move on, you will find some challenges along the way. The narcissist in your life will not be very happy about it, as you might already be guessing, and will look for extra hurtful ways to keep you feeling bad about yourself and happy to make you feel like you are doing something wrong. Don't take the bait.

A narcissist needs people to love them and follow them without question so they might bad-mouth you to your mutual friends and allies, leaving you feeling concerned that all of those people will think you are a bad person and have done something wrong, clearly crazy to be letting go of such an amazing person. Don't fall for it.

All of these traps will be designed to make you feel like you don't know what you are doing, that you are making a mistake and that you aren't going to get a better life, no matter what you might be telling yourself.

All of these manipulation tactics are designed to urge you to stay in the patterns of behavior designed by the narcissist who just needs you to be at their beck and call. Forgive, forget, and move on.

These four suggestions can help you refrain from falling back into the patterns and continue with your growth journey as you choose to detach from your partnership:

1. Refuse to Fall for the Old Tricks

They are amazingly convincing and charming when they know they have to maintain their reality. Hold your convictions, and don't let their old tricks sway you and keep you from walking out the door and into the life you are hoping for.

2. Determine Your Limits

Narcissists have no empathy and are not capable of the love you think they are, so you may need just to cut the cord, painful as it may feel at first, and move on. Setting limits and telling them no, either out loud or in your mind and heart, will help you know that you have set limits with this relationship and that it is no longer a good choice for you. Determining the limits of your relationship will help you gather strength to let go and move on.

3. Think About Your Future

To help you get out of your situation and also to prevent you from going back if they "win you over" with their manipulation tactics, focus on your future without them and how you want it to be. Consider all of the opportunities you will have and how good it will feel to have some freedom and a chance to heal from your experience where you can rekindle the most important relationship in your life: your relationship with yourself.

4. Offer Yourself Kindness and Self-Love

The habit when coming out of a relationship with a narcissist might be to cut yourself down, accuse yourself, or blame yourself for the relationship not working out. Your self-worth might be lowered from experience, and you may be feeling less than adequate as a partner and as a person. To help yourself feel more empowered about your choice to let go and move on, give all the love you would be giving to your partner to yourself. You can give yourself the love you deserve, and now is the perfect time to start.

Every relationship we experience helps us to grow. You haven't failed by being in a relationship with a narcissistic person. If anything, you have learned more about what you are willing to endure for love and what you are no longer willing to sacrifice at the expense of yourself. A relationship like this can show you how to create boundaries, how to say "no" to someone, and how to determine when you are letting go of yourself to make someone else happy.

Healthy partnerships will be more accessible for you after you have learned how to be open and honest about your wants, needs, and desires, unlike how you were involved in the narcissistic partnership. Don't "beat yourself up" for having had a relationship that caused you such issues or problems. The most important thing right now is that you continue to improve your life after identifying what those issues are and how to survive that experience to enjoy a happier, healthier relationship in the future.

All of this might look and sound great on paper, but when it comes to the reality of leaving a relationship, it isn't just as easy and simple as following a few guidelines. Often in life, we need more help than that, and it is available to us when we ask for it and start to tell our stories.

Chapter 7

Recovering from A Relationship
Whit A Narcissist

The first stage of narcissistic abuse recovery is emergency stabilization. In this stage, the victim suffers overstimulation from their abuser. Even if the victim has been able to cut the abuser out of their life, the narcissist is still everywhere. The narcissist is still in their thoughts. Their abuser's negativity is still dragging them down. The victim walks on eggshells, trying to keep their abuser happy.

The victim might feel uncomfortable in quite normal moments. They no longer have to worry about the needs of their partner. Their partner's needs might have gone above everything else in the relationship. They may feel lost and unsure of what to do with their time. They do not feel confident enough to trust themselves with making any decisions. The victim might find themselves struggling to make basic choices like what to eat.

In this stage, life might be a haze. The victim has low energy, and they struggle to complete a task, such as taking care of the children. Self-care is important in this stage. The victim should focus their time and energy to take a shower, eat a balanced meal, and get rest. The victim might not feel like eating, or they might want to stress eat. The victim might want to sleep all the time or stay awake all night due to anxiety. The focus now should be finding a healthy balance.

Another thing the victim could do to help heal is journaling. Journaling is a judgment-free way of expelling all the negativity that has built up inside. In a journal, a person can write how they are feeling and thinking. The writing can bring bad habits and patterns out into the light. Writing also has a way of bringing a person to the present. A person's mind gets stuck in the past after a bad breakup.

It is important to stay without contact with the narcissist. If it is impossible for the victim to go without contact, the victim should use a technique called grey rock. Grey rock is interacting with the narcissist in a way where they are emotionally and mentally disengaged. In other words, stay calm.

The victim should destroy or give away all items that bring up memories of the narcissist. The items include photos and gifts, as they will bring up nostalgic memories, making it harder to let go.

Stage two of recovery is punching upward. In this stage, the victim moves out of the fog, where the narcissist left them. They will still be uncertain of their own choices, but the victim will start to regain some of their energy. In this stage, it is not uncommon for the person to feel surges of anger at the narcissist and themselves for allowing the abuse to go on for a long time.

It is important that the victims recognize that anger is a natural part of the healing process. The anger that the victim feels is righteous anger.

Righteous anger is what one may feel when someone does something against them. Its purpose is to move the person into action. Once the person has acted by leaving a dangerous relationship, for example, the anger left can cause bad side effects. It is important that the victim recognizes that it is okay to feel angry and lets that anger go.

The victim should properly process the anger. One way to process the anger is to set apart some time alone in a safe place to face it. In this space, the victim can scream, cry, or punch a pillow to release some of the anger.

Exercise is a healthy outlet to release anger. Some good exercise choices are jogging, cardio, and kickboxing because they get the person up and moving. Creative expressions like dance, music, and art can be healthy outlets.

The feeling of blame, shame, and guilt can be toxic to recovery, but these feelings are difficult to get rid of. The victim has lived years being the target of the narcissist's blame. The victim might be questioning why they left. If they had worked harder, would the relationship have worked?

The first step to getting rid of the blame is to look inward and let go. The victim should take a critical look at themselves and ask if they are really to blame. This self-scrutiny might be too hard for the victim to accomplish at first.

A narcissistic relationship is different than healthy relationships. The victim is not responsible for any of the abuse that they have faced. The victim needs to realize that and let go of all the guilt. A big step toward doing this might be educating themselves on narcissistic abuse.

The victim should not just forget the hurt of the past, but they should take what they can learn from the experience and leave the rest. If a person forgets the past, they are likely to make the same mistakes again. In this case, the victim might go back to their abuser or find a different abuser. Instead of blaming themselves for ignoring the red flags in their past relationship, they should remember what happened when they ignored them. The victim will have this knowledge for entering relationships in the future.

The third stage is the one-foot-out-the-door stage. The victim begins to rebuild their identity. They feel more confident about the decisions that they make. In this stage, the victim might start to reminisce about their ex. They may not believe that things were as bad as they remembered. They may be curious as to how their ex is doing without them.

Reconnection with the narcissist is not a good idea. When the victim tries to reconnect, they can get sucked into the abusive situation again. The victim can also relapse into the first or second stage of recovery.

The narcissist might turn on the charm and try to remind the victim why they loved them. They will use the love that the victim felt like an emotional hook to pull them back in. The narcissist might also meet the victim coldly.

The abuser might verbally abuse the victim and brag about how much better they are now that they are out of the relationship. The reaction from the narcissist can leave the victim hurt and confused. Nothing good comes from getting back in touch.

A closure is something that a narcissist cannot give. A closure demands that the person understands that their actions affect other people. The person has to be able to empathize. When a victim tries to get closer, they are feeding into the narcissist's supply. The fact they managed to hurt the victim boosts their self-esteem.

Gaining self-confidence after experiencing narcissistic abuse will take some time. The narcissist has stripped everything from the victim. They may no longer know what they want or feel comfortable in their own skin.

An important step into rebuilding themselves is to surround themselves with positive people. The victim should take this opportunity to make all the negative people leave their life. If the victim's sister always criticizes their every movement, then it's time to distance themselves from their sister.

The victim should invite new positive people into their life, especially those who are supportive. The victim might be skeptical of other people, as it can take a while to trust anyone again.

Volunteering is a good excuse to get out of the house. When a person volunteers, they are serving others. Volunteering might feel a need that drew the narcissists to the victim. The act of volunteering might help the victim understand what they want to do with their life. If they volunteer with animals, they might decide to be a vet. If the person reads to children, they might decide to be a teacher.

The victim should avoid comparing themselves to others. They should instead focus on personal achievements, as comparison leads to negative self-talk. It might make the victim forget that it takes time to rebuild their life.

One good way to rebuild self-esteem is to set small goals and accomplish them. The goals need to be meaningful and something easy to track. A small goal might be to walk once a week or get dressed each day.

Getting dressed every day will help the victim feel better. Smiling will also make the victim feel better because it releases endorphins into their brain. If the victim looks and acts as if they have confidence, it will help them rebuild it.

The fourth stage of recovery is objective analysis. In this phase, the victim can look into the past without feeling angry. The victim has learned how to look inward and identify emotional triggers. There may be times when the victim slides back into feelings of worthlessness and doubt.

Take this situation as an example. The victim goes shopping one day years after they have left their abusive situation. All of a sudden, the victim starts to feel as if they can't breathe, their palms are sweaty, and their heartbeat quickens. The victim leaves the store and later feels better. The victim is left confused about what had happened in the store.

Emotional triggers are things that make the victim feel that they are back into an abusive situation. People who suffered from narcissistic abuse can have flashbacks like people with post-traumatic stress do. Certain things trigger the fight or flight reflex, and the victim might suffer a panic attack or feel ill.

The triggers are different for everyone. The triggers are things that remind the person about the time before, during, or soon after the abuse. When a person first leaves an abusive situation, they do not know what their emotional triggers are. It takes a while to learn about them. If the person isn't aware of emotional triggers, the effects can be scary and confusing. The triggers could set the victim back in their path to recovery.

The triggers are linked to a person's five senses. The trigger could be something that a person sees, including someone who resembles the abuser or something that reminds them of the abuser, such as clothing or style. If the victim sees someone who mimics the body language of their victims, such as crossed arms or a raised eyebrow, it might trigger anxiety or stress. An item that reminds the victim of when they lived with the narcissist can be a trigger. Another trigger could be an item of abuse, such as when the abuser hit the victim with a belt or a ruler so that such items could trigger stress.

The trigger could also be something that the person hears. The song or group of songs that their abuser liked to listen to could put them right back into the abuse. The abuser's favorite T.V. show or movie could also be strong triggers. The victim could feel stressed if they hear angry or loud words, as well. Another sound that could be a stressor is a word or phrase that the victim said a lot. If the abuser had a habit of calling the victim "doll," then that nickname might make them feel uneasy now.

Another trigger is smelling specific scents, such as the cologne or body wash they used, or the abuser's body odor could become triggers. The smell of cigarettes, alcohol, or favorite food could bother the victim, too. The smell of the house they shared, air freshener, or bleach could all bring the victim back to the past.

The taste of the abuser's favorite food or the food that they ate a lot during the time of the abuse could trigger flashbacks. It is possible that a person could feel ill when they eat foods that they once loved if they reminded the victim of their abuser.

Chapter 8

Co-parenting with A Narcissist

There are two things you can do to co-parent with a narcissist in a moment of frustration successfully.

Document all conversations while trying to keep a minimal amount of interaction. Download a parenting app where everything is organized and "businesslike" and have all conversations go through this app. This allows both of you to keep the focus on your child, as well as have a shared record of all communication, dates, visitation, etc. If this is unavailable or the narcissist does not want to cooperate in this way, create a planner or journal where you can keep your own notes. By doing this, you can have information and recorded data in case things escalate to having to go to court to fight for your children. All conversations must be professional, straight forward, and if at all, it starts to lead to an argument, you have the power to end it. If you don't trust yourself to stay under control, have someone you trust with you to be the mediator and defuse a situation or calm you down if need be.

Create an organized parenting plan. The moment you officially call your partnership over, make sure that you set up a parenting plan. It's best to have a lawyer or a mediator present to help with this process. A narcissist will rarely abuse you when someone else is around – unless they are malignant. Be sure the parenting plan is very specific, as a narcissist will look for any loopholes to trap you and gaslight you about what was agreed upon. Markdown which days (not weekends) each parent will have their child, who will have primary care, and what should happen on holidays. Explain how transportation will be handled, where and who to communicate if an emergency happens, etc. If you have an organized parenting plan, it will help minimize conversation between you and the narcissist, as you both will know the plan.

"What if I lose control?" Many co-parents have this fear when ending their relationship with a narcissist. We are all human, and it's the narcissist's goal to get a rise out of you so they can use it against you in any way they can. Staying in control is a must, so here are some ideas on how to maintain your composure.

You are in charge of you – Accept what cannot be changed and move on. During the relationship, your control and sense of self-identity may have been taken from you; however, you realize that you control your own actions. You have always had this ability, and you always will. It doesn't matter what they do, say, react to, or think because it is not you or the way you believe things to be.

With that being said, let go of what the narcissistic parent does with your child as you will have your own rules and structure. The more you engage with everything they are doing wrong for your child, the more you feed into the narcissist's desire to spite you. For example, even if you put your child to bed at eight in the evening, they may choose to put them to bed at ten or let them stay awake all night. Put aside your beliefs about what they should do and do your best to maintain a healthy environment for your kids.

Be a good role model – All the things you wish your child to obtain and hold as a healthy, independent individual, you should model. Be empathetic, kind, compassionate, understanding, supportive, forgiving, etc.

Whichever emotions or behaviors your child will not learn from the narcissistic parent, make them prominent in your time with your little ones. Give them guidance, structure, discipline, and protection in your attempts to have them grow up into decent human beings. Show your child that it is okay to love yourself while at the same time feeling compassion and love for someone else. Teach them what it means to have empathy for someone while being assertive is also their right.

Have a community backing you – All difficult things are easier said than done. The struggle is that the narcissist will try everything from manipulating you into feeling guilty for being a parent, convincing you that they are the better parent, or even trying to win you back to get you on their side again. Every narcissistic co-parenting situation is different. As a narcissist is only out for themselves, they are not hurt by the breakup – they just want to belittle you, drag you down, and have you question all your parenting or personal abilities to handle this situation. They will not care how it affects your child, just knowing that you are suffering makes them feel united and at peace with themselves. The more you show sadness, weakness, or feed into this behavior, the more you are letting them regain their power over you. By having a strong and supportive community behind you, you can get the guidance and positive feedback or criticism that you need always to do your best. This community of people can include your close, trusted friends, family members, and therapists.

The most important thing when co-parenting with a narcissist is to let go of what they say and do and focus on yourself and your child. Basically, act as if you don't have them in you or your child's lives. Maybe it's easier to convince yourself that your children are going to their grandparents for visits. Do not fake your reality, but take on only the stress that shows up in your personal life – not the stress the narcissist tries to make you suffer with.

How to Give the Best Guidance to Your Child – You have learned that they will continue to do things to spite you, manipulate you or your children, and always have their own best interests at heart – not your child's. By limiting contact, setting parental guidelines, providing structure for yourself, modeling healthy communication, and ignoring the narcissist's attempts to abuse you, you can focus more on your child. In this co-parenting situation, your child's development is of crucial importance.

The first thing you must do for your child is to foster healthy qualities which include:

1. Encourage individuality

Children are influenced by everything and everyone in their world. A narcissist will make them believe that they have to please everyone or "bow down" to their peers in order to feel loved or appreciated. The child of a narcissist is not an individual, but a reflection of them. You, being the non-narcissistic parent, can counteract these habits by helping your child realize that they are their own person. Seek opportunities for your child to grow independently, such as:

- Providing creative activities
- Asking them which sports or summer camp they would like to join
- Journaling their thoughts and feelings
- Letting them choose their own clothes and toys

2. Encourage self-esteem

Self-esteem is built through unconditional love and acknowledgment. Build positive reinforcement through the milestones your child accomplishes in their lives. Give them praise when it's needed, not when they do something to gain your affection. Narcissists have a high, self-absorbed image and so their love will only ever be conditional as long as your child serves them and their needs. More ways to counteract this are:

- Tell your child that they are smart or good (when they are good) to remind them that they have good traits.

- Praise them for things like going potty on their own, winning third place at the fair, or displaying good behavior with their friends.
- Be careful with what you say to them, e.g., "you are so awesome in my eyes" rather than "you are the most awesome person in the whole wide world."

3. Help build self-confidence

Narcissists deny their children self-confidence when they praise them only for their worth to the narcissist. Simply put, they tell their children that they are only worthy and accepted IF they behave this way or think that way. Your child is always taking in new information and building skills so, to boost their self-confidence, reward them by saying things like "wow, you are really good at that, show me again." Or "some things take practice, why don't we try again?" In doing this, you allow your child to figure out what their strengths and weaknesses are, which encourages independence and teaches them to develop confidence in the things they can do while letting go of perfecting what they can't. Try this:

- Sign your child up for a sports team
- Encourage them to try new things
- Explain that being fearful is their body's way of reacting to change and that change is a good thing

4. Allow mistakes to be opportunities

A narcissistic parent will make sure that their child strives to be the best and only rewards them when they are the best. This promotes perfectionism and results in temper tantrums when your child can't impress. Teach your child:

- Mistakes will happen but are needed to grow into happy individuals.

- Make a mistake on purpose in front of your child, and don't make it a big deal. E.g., paint together and "accidentally" the color out of the lines. Say oops and laugh about it.

- Challenge them to things they don't enjoy doing or are not good at doing, then applaud their efforts and say "good job for trying."

- Do not exaggerate their accomplishments, as focusing too much on this can put pressure on them, which encourages perfectionist behavior.

5. Create positive influences and environments for your child

Creating a stable environment for your child – one where they will feel safe, secure, and confident – will keep their minds at ease during the switch between parents. As hard as this is on you to co-parent with your ex, it is even harder on your children to adapt to such change. This can also help your child make positive connections and learn from others – not just you. It's best to remember that you are not perfect – you are only human, and you, as a parent, will make mistakes. These mistakes may be that you lash out in anger in front of your child (not towards them), call your ex down by accident when talking to friends, or break down under all the pressure. In fact, these mistakes are needed so that your child can see that you are not perfect, either. They will see that it's okay to make mistakes, as long as we can try to fix them or move forward from them. In all your best efforts as the non-narcissistic parent to develop positive traits into your child, you may not be able to stop the narcissistic traits that may already be developed into them.

So, the second step is to counteract the narcissistic traits of your child. You can do this by:

1. Teaching your child empathy All children and teens are selfish individuals, as this is part of their development to independence and individuality. However, it doesn't become a problem unless there is no remorse or feelings behind their actions. You can teach them empathy by

   - Always remind them that other people have feelings, too.
   - When reading or watching TV, ask your child how they think the person feels.
   - When your child does something good or bad to someone else, ask them how they would feel if it had been done to them. This will help them realize the other person's feelings.

2. Explaining the importance of friends and family, Narcissists are usually lonely and sheltered. They rarely have friends come over, and they rarely let their child have play dates.

That is because narcissists become envious of their children's relationships when they don't have any.

Chapter 9

Recommended Activities for Recovery

Though you can do a lot to prompt your recovery by reading, as you are doing, at some point, you need to leave your comfort zone and establish your recovery by being active with your body.

If you are already the athletic type, you may need to find greater challenges. If you already go for daily walks and/or runs and do yoga, your recovery might require a more drastic alteration in your activity level.

The point is that it is important to be active in order to recover. If you don't put your body in motion, it will never be in motion. If it never is in motion, it will never stay in motion. Don't get stuck. Your relationship with a narcissist was all about making you feel stuck. You felt tied to them. You felt tied to their approval.

You felt tied to doing things their way. Now, you need to pursue your own activities actively. Right now, depending on your stage of recovery, going for a walk every day and doing a few yoga poses before bed might make a world of difference.

If you already think that you will need more than a walk or some yoga to prompt your recovery, you may want to join some sort of trendy fitness group that will really get you going and challenge you in healthy ways.

Maybe you need to start doing cross-fit or Pilates. Maybe you need to teach fitness classes again. Maybe you need to go back to doing whatever kind of fitness the narcissist in your life put down. If the narcissist you were in a relationship thought yoga was bullshit, yoga might be exactly what you need to do to prompt your recovery and regain control.

Keep in mind that walks and yoga are good supplements, however. The following activities might not be sufficient for you, but that doesn't mean they aren't beneficial. Part of the reason for these activities is to make you feel like you're actively part of the world again (not just the world of the narcissist you were with).

Part of the reason for these activities is to help you learn how to relax again. Think about how often the narcissist you were with wanted you to relax. Think about how much the narcissist you were with affected your approach to relaxation.

It might be necessary for you to reevaluate how you feel about relaxation. One thing worth keeping in mind as you approach these activities is that their purpose is to help you relax because relaxation is a key component for recovery.

Going on Walks

Going on walks is excellent for recovery; age does not matter. If some aid is necessary, use one. Whether you're single and need to spend some time walking alone or with a partner, a walk is a good way to process the day. Partners should go on walks to talk about their lives and to observe the seasons together.

Walks inspire questions about nature, which makes us turn our gaze outward. We get to step away from ourselves, which gives us the kind of distance that is necessary for recovery. Walks are an opportunity for you to teach yourself nature. If you come up with questions you do not have the answer to, you should make it a project for yourself to discover the answer.

One activity while walking is to observe the trees and the effects of the seasonal changes. If you walk frequently enough, you will be able to bear witness to the changes of the seasons. Observe the changes in the leaves if there are leaves.

If it is winter, consider what the absence of leaves means for the animals and insects that spend time in trees. Get outside of yourself on these walks. Getting outside of yourself and into nature will give you a new perspective on yourself the next time you take a look inward.

A second activity is journaling. You could bring along a notepad or journal and write down questions you have about plants, animals, and trees you see. The other day my mother and I struggled to recall the name for Spanish Broom.

It took up much of the conversation along our walk. We were pleased when she finally recalled the name for the lovely bushes filled with fragrant yellow flowers that appear to have bloomed late this year.

A third activity is stopping to smell the roses. Actually, it is stopping to take a closer look at anything that inspires interest at all. Make the mission of a walk the walk itself, not the conclusion of a walk. Find enjoyment in the journey. Take breaks. Stop and see. Stop and smell. Stop and touch. Stop and talk.

It is important to get away from yourself by looking at nature but also important to remember to look inward from time to time.

You might learn interesting things about yourself by noticing what makes you stop in order to get a closer look.

The difference is that this activity also encourages you to ask why you stopped to investigate a particular thing. This is a cause for self-reflection. Why does the Spanish Broom interest you more than the mailbox next to it? Or is it the cat in the window that has your attention?

A fifth activity is observing the weather. An obvious start is assessing the current weather activity. A more in-depth analysis is asking what purposes changes in weather might mean on a cosmic level.

The narcissist you were in a relationship made you feel small so that they could feel big. When you think about the cosmos, no human being stands as tall as the narcissist made you think they did. Thinking about the cosmos debunks the myth, they tried to make you believe about their greatness.

A sixth activity is skipping. It has come to my intention that fewer and fewer people know the joys of skipping. It is essential to check in on one's coordination. Skipping is often as fun as it is fundamentally useful in developing one's motor skills. Skip to acknowledging the rhythm of your body as it moves in accordance with the ground below it, resisting and accepting the pull of gravity.

A seventh activity is jumping over the cracks in the sidewalk. Part of developing mindfulness and self-awareness is making an activity out of awareness of one's surroundings and interaction with one's surroundings. Jumping over cracks in the sidewalk makes one aware of the ground one walks on.

It's perfectly understandable if civilization has made you too embarrassed to do skip or jump over cracks. Find a private place for these activities in that case. Or, if you have a child, do these activities with them. It will be good for both of you.

An eighth activity is listening. Walking and talking is great, but silence during a walk is advantageous, too. Challenge yourself to listen to your surroundings. Then, if you're on an accompanied walk, invite talking once more and discuss what you heard.

A ninth activity is closing your eyes and trying to remember what your surroundings are. Walk to a certain spot and stop. Cover your eyes and recall what you've just seen in front of you. If you begin to get good at this activity, start asking yourself to remember what is to the left of you, right of you, and behind you.

A tenth activity follows the walk. Put your arms above your head and breathe deeply. Try to relax more with every breath. Learning how to relax is one of the most important parts of your recovery. Narcissists are often exciting and energizing because they need so much of you.

It can become addicting to feel that you must never relax because of this. So, in order to recover, you must learn to relax. Yoga, when properly practiced, is a helpful way to relax, meditate, and recover from just about anything.

Playing with Yoga Poses

Yoga poses are cleverly and playfully named to attach themselves to natural poses found in nature. Some of them refer to human poses, such as Dancer and Happy Baby. Others refer to animals, such as Downward Dog and Pigeon. Doing these poses creates body-awareness. Here are ten yoga poses that have been said to promote healing.

One pose is Child's Pose. Allowing your lungs to expand improves the flow of oxygen to your brain. The child's pose is a resting pose. It is best to rest and to breathe in a child's pose. In the child's pose, your shins, palms, and forehead rest on the ground. Your spine curves. Your chest rests on the top of your thighs. If you have any knee or hip issues, spread your knees farther apart.

A second pose is Hero's Pose (Virasana). Leaving your legs as they are in Child's pose, lengthen your upper body and rise until the crown of your head is directly above your hips, and your spine is straight.

Breath deeply and allow the shoulders to fall. Keep reaching the crown of the head to the sky. Consider the names of the poses. Consider if you feel safe or vulnerable in Child's Pose. Consider if you feel powerful in Hero's Pose. Be mindful of your body. Be mindful of yourself. A third pose is Mountain Pose (Tadasana). Mountain Pose is a powerful pose. Rise from the ground, from Child's Pose and Hero's pose, and stand tall. Continue reaching the crown of the head to the sky but with the full extension of your legs supporting you now. Open the palms to receive energy. Close your eyes. As we age, sitting in Child's Pose and Hero's Pose can be strenuous if our muscles are tight in certain places. You should not have this issue in Mountain Pose. The struggle you might run into in Mountain Pose is losing your balance once your eyes are closed. Acknowledge the connection between the functioning of your body and your sense perception. Find your balance. Maintain it as long as you can. A fourth pose is Tree Pose (Vriksasana). From Mountain Pose, you can practice balancing on one leg. First, play with the foot that will remain on the ground. See how well you can spread your toes. The wider you spread your toes, the more rooted you will be to the ground. Once you have rooted yourself with the foot you will stand on, begin to lift the other foot. It is totally fine if you are unable to place your foot on the inside of your thigh. Start by trying to place the toes of your lifted foot on the ankle of your grounded foot. If you find this to be quite easy, keep inching the lifted foot higher. The goal is to get the toes of the lifted foot above the knee of the rooted leg. The inside of your lifted leg should face forward, creating a figure-four with your legs. Once you are satisfied with your attempts on one leg, do the other!

Chapter 10

Healing the Patterns

After the storm, when the waves of the emotional seas calm down a little bit, and you can feel a new attitude and outlook on your life, you may still have a lot of work to do to help yourself recover from your awakened awareness of the situation.

When you are in a narcissistic abuse situation, the best recourse is to remove yourself from gaining insight. Surviving a narcissistic relationship and staying with a partner who has this personality disorder can be a very one-sided battle that you will fight alone, and you will have to decide what is most important for you in your relationship with yourself.

Even if you have ties that keep you together, like children or other matters, you can still succeed and thrive after the storm has calmed, and you have moved forward and onward. To fully heal from the cycles of abuse, the toxic patterns of narcissistic partnership, and the emotional manipulation you endured, you will have to do a lot of personal growth work to support your choice and remove any doubts in making the right choice. Being mentally manipulated for some time is not without its damaging side-effects, and it could take some time for you to end the emotional upheaval you experienced.

The person you were involved with may still try to convince you that you have something special and that you are making a huge mistake, or you may find yourself head over heels with another partner soon after you end your relationship, who also happens to be a narcissist, but you weren't able to see the red flags because of how close you still are to those behaviors, thoughts, and emotional patterns.

After You Walk Away

After you walk away from a narcissistic partnership, you may go through several feelings of doubt, uncertainty, "but what-ifs," and all sorts of highs and lows that will want you to question whether or not you have made the right choice. You will always have to work out your version of what happened in your relationship with your partner, and they are not going to be willing or able to face the trauma you experienced. Your narcissistic partner won't even care that you are or were in pain or that you felt emotionally abused, and so anything that comes up and suggests that you are doing something wrong or making the wrong choice by leaving your partner is just more of the toxic reality of being a victim of narcissistic abuse rearing its head.

The following guidelines will help you stay focused on getting through the hard parts of walking away and how to continue healing the patterns of the narcissistic relationship and cycles of abuse.

1. Process your emotions.

Spending time with your feelings, honoring them, labeling them, and acknowledging your experiences and the events of your relationship will help you manage the reality of what you experienced more efficiently and effectively. When you can explore what happened from a distance, instead of from the confines of the relationship, you will have a clearer perspective. You can even try to imagine how it would look if it happened to someone else, like a friend or a colleague, to help you see more objectively and process your feelings from a variety of angles.

Using a journal or notebook, seeking counseling, and asking for support in a group can also help you process your emotions more effectively so that you don't have floods of feelings or doubts about your process as you change course and create a new life for yourself.

2. Keep it personal, and try not to generalize.

It would be very easy to become cynical and embittered about anyone in the world after an experience of narcissistic abuse, and creating a shield of armor to prevent further issues can be even more damaging. The tendency might be to generalize the situation to say, "all women are control freaks," or "all men are manipulative masochists," but that is simply not the case or the answer to your healing dialogue. Take time to reflect on the situation as a personal experience and not the assumption of all society, all men, all women, or all of anything.

3. A little self-compassion goes a long way.

You may no longer be offering yourself compassion. How could you be after living with a narcissist who is the antithesis of compassion and empathy? Pitying yourself or being overly critical of your experience will keep you locked in patterns of self-abuse, the learned behavior of emotional manipulation you gained in your relationship. The antidote to those feelings is self-compassion, which could take some practice at first, but a little goes a long way and will add up over time, supporting you in a much healthier way.

Be kind and try not to judge yourself too much. Be understanding that you are not a fool for getting involved with someone like that; they are incredibly charming and warm when you first get to know them and incredibly skilled at convincing you of anything. You are not an idiot or a fool. So, just be kind and understanding in the face of the narcissistic aftermath.

Recognize that thousands of people find themselves in these circumstances and that you are one of many people who were a victim of narcissistic abuse.

4. The high-road is the road to take.

Reacting to your narcissistic ex is not always easy to avoid, especially when they are provoking you and looking for a fight just to prove a point. Take the high road in every situation. It may feel awkward and uncomfortable at the moment because you have to put with their antics, but you will find a sense of relief, calm, and responsibility for your emotional agility when you choose the path that reflects a more grounded, resourceful, and wise individual.

Everything in recovery and moving forward is a stepping stone. It may feel like a long-haul, but every choice that you make every day to help yourself let go and move forward healthily is what takes you to the path you truly want to be on, as you create a happier and more fulfilling life for yourself.

Know the Flags

A great way to keep yourself out of the patterns of narcissistic coupling and abuse is to make sure you know and understand what all of the flags are.

If you are recovering from this type of a relationship, you will be much more likely to spot a flag from a mile away, but even still, narcissists can be incredibly cunning and slippery and are willing to do whatever it takes to convince you they are 100 percent compatible with you.

Researching your experience and finding out all of the specific experiences as you process, journal, and speak to a therapist will help you prevent a future narcissistic relationship. Watch out for the following flags as you meet new people and embrace new romances:

- Idolizing you in front of friends and family to an extreme degree

- Love-bombing

- Whirlwind getaways in a very short time

- Promising things and not sticking to those promises

- Having manic episodes of extreme love expressions (think Tom Cruise jumping onto Oprah's sofa)

- Excessive sexual needs

- The subtle devaluing of your efforts or feelings

- Not taking the blame for anything

- Never apologizing

- Expecting your love without offering much in return

This list is just the beginning before things get worse, and you don't want them to get worse, so heading it off at the pass with these first few red flags is a good plan.

Seek Help

You are not alone, and many people have experienced or are experiencing what you are going through. Don't be afraid to ask for help and find a support system to offer you what you need to stay balanced, secure, and self-confident in your choices and journey forward.

It has never been your fault that the person you are in a relationship with doesn't understand their disorder or issue, and even if you were capable of enabling it for a long period of time, you are certainly capable of healing from it and learning how not to repeat the same patterns over and over again.

Help is always available and all around you. If you cannot get to a public support group, or feel comfortable talking to friends and family about it, go online and look for more resources. Find an anonymous group to join if you want to protect your identity. Ask other people what it was like for them and how their recovery process is going. You will learn so much by simply reaching out for help and letting it clear your fears that you are somehow at fault for your experience.

All it takes is awareness and courage, as you let go of the narcissistic relationship. Empowering yourself to enjoy your life more through a balanced partnership is what any person deserves, and you are on the right track to getting there. Heal the patterns so that they are broken and cannot be repeated by offering yourself kindness, staying personal with your journey, process your emotions regularly, take the high road, know the red flags of the narcissist, and seek help whenever you feel like you need support.

You are on your way to becoming the confident, happy, and balanced person you always knew you are and could be. Learning to survive the narcissistic relationship may seem hard at first, but you have all of the tools that you need to accept your story and begin the healing journey.

Conclusion.

Narcissists are difficult to get along with. You're probably already familiar with the self-centeredness, grandiosity, vanity, and vulnerability that characterize this problematic personality style. You've been idealized, devalued, taken for granted, and taken advantage of. Where do you go from here?

Narcissism is a condition that robs people of their personhood. It reduces everyone (both the narcissist and the people they care about) to objects that are defined by superficial qualities. The only antidote is to do the hard work of finding the real people behind the projections. This book shared some insights into better understanding yourself and the narcissist in your life, and provided the information you need to make an informed choice about what to do with that relationship.

This book attempted to give you the tools to decode and unmask narcissistic behaviors. It discussed stories that illustrate how narcissistic traits can look in real-life scenarios, and reviewed exercises to help you clarify your thoughts, feelings, and values. It also covered setting boundaries, confronting and accepting vulnerability, and finding balance within yourself.

Narcissists use grandiosity as a defense against insecurity, shame, and vulnerability, attempting to offload negative feelings onto others through denial and projection. Although the temptation is to throw those negative feelings back at the narcissist, doing so only exacerbates anger and tension. Instead of going to war with the narcissist's projections, being able to acknowledge and accept your own vulnerabilities will allow you to remain centered in response to narcissistic devaluation.

Self-centered behaviors like entitlement, low empathy, and exploitation are traits narcissists use to make up for deep feelings of impoverishment. On an emotional level, narcissists are starving and desperate for your help. If you let them, they will gobble up all of your resources, leaving you to starve as well. Set boundaries to protect your emotional and psychological space. Be assertive, keeping in mind the differences between aggressive, passive, and assertive behavior. Perhaps most importantly, don't get too attached to outcomes. All you can do is speak your truth. If someone doesn't respect your boundaries, you always have the choice to walk away.

Finally, with vanity, narcissists try to create a perfect outside to compensate for an emotionally chaotic inside. Using the concept of splitting, narcissists tend to unconsciously separate themselves and the world into categories of perfect and worthless, good and bad, idealized and devalued. Since narcissists' extreme thoughts and feelings often create complimentary extreme thoughts and feelings in others, it can help to monitor your own inner experience to avoid being pulled into splitting. Narcissism cuts people up into good and bad pieces. The best way to confront this is to approach things as a whole, complex person.

If you decide to continue working on your relationship with the narcissist in your life, consider enlisting support. Family and friends can be great resources when you need a reminder that you aren't alone. You might also consider talking to a therapist. Therapy isn't just for people with severe mental health issues. It can be a tremendous source of support when dealing with stressful situations. Therapists are trained to meet you where you are, offering appropriate and individually tailored feedback to help you better understand yourself and your situation. A good therapist will listen in an attentive and nonreactive way, providing feedback that gives you a feeling of being seen and understood. Sometimes, it takes a few tries before finding a good match.

If the narcissist in your life is open to the idea, she might also benefit from therapy. Just be careful not to use the idea of therapy as a weapon. It's easy to say things like, "You *really* need therapy!" or "You have issues. Why don't you go see a shrink?" These sorts of comments are really just ways of throwing negative projections back at the narcissist. It is counterproductive because it reinforces the stereotype that therapy is only for "crazy" people. It also stigmatizes seeking help as something shameful (and narcissists are not huge fans of feeling shame). Instead, wait for a calm moment and express your encouragement in an open and caring way. You might say, "You know, I hear you talking about how stressed you've been feeling lately. Have you considered getting some support from a therapist? I think talking to an expert might really help you feel better about things."

This journey began with the myth of Narcissus, who tragically fell in love with an ideal image of himself too perfect to ever exist in the real world. Equally tragic is the story of Echo, whose voice was never heard by the preoccupied Narcissus. While you may be playing the part of Echo at this moment, you don't have to allow yourself to be eclipsed by the Narcissus in your life. Although difficult, it is possible to work toward making enough space for both you and the other person to "show up" to each other. Even if the narcissist in your life isn't willing to make changes, you have the ability to make yourself better, give yourself the space and consideration that you deserve, and make sure that your voice is heard. Sometimes this is a journey that you can take *with* the narcissist in your life. Sometimes it isn't. Either way, don't lose sight of your right to be heard, respected, and seen.